The Sweetness of Life

Françoise Héritier

Translated by Anthea Bell

PARTICULAR BOOKS
an imprint of
PENGUIN BOOKS

PARTICULAR BOOKS

Published by the Penguin Group
Penguin Books Ltd, 80 Strand, London WC2R ORL, England
Penguin Group (USA) Inc., 375 Hudson Street, New York, New York 10014, USA
Penguin Group (Canada), 90 Eglinton Avenue East, Suite 700,
Toronto, Ontario, Canada M4P 2Y3 (a division of Pearson Penguin Canada Inc.)
Penguin Ireland, 25 St Stephen's Green, Dublin 2, Ireland (a division of Penguin Books Ltd)
Penguin Group (Australia), 707 Collins Street, Melbourne, Victoria 3008, Australia
(a division of Pearson Australia Group Pty Ltd)
Penguin Books India Pvt Ltd, 11 Community Centre, Panchsheel Park,
New Delhi – 110 017, India
Penguin Group (NZ), 67 Apollo Drive, Rosedale, North Shore 0632, New Zealand
(a division of Pearson New Zealand Ltd)
Penguin Books (South Africa) (Pty) Ltd, Block D, Rosebank Office Park, 181 Jan Smuts Avenue, Parktown
North, Gauteng 2193, South Africa

Penguin Books Ltd, Registered Offices: 80 Strand, London WC2R ORL, England

www.penguin.com

First published as *Le Sel de la Vie* by Odile Jacob, 2012
Published in Great Britain by Particular Books 2013
1

Copyright © Odile Jacob, 2012
Translation copyright © Anthea Bell, 2013

The moral right of the author and the translator has been asserted

Set in Granjon Lt Std 13.75/16.5pt
Typeset by Claire Mason
Printed in Great Britain by Clays Ltd, St Ives plc

A CIP catalogue record for this book is available from the British Library

978-1-846-14699-2

www.greenpenguin.co.uk

Penguin Books is committed to a sustainable
future for our business, our readers and our
planet. This book is made from paper certified
by the Forest Stewardship Council.

ALWAYS LEARNING

Introduction

The following text will surprise those who know me from my anthropological writings. In all humility, I claim that this is another of them: a 'fantasy' born of my pen and inspiration – and it has a story behind it. One fine summer's day, if I may be allowed that expression, since the weather was appalling, I had a postcard from Scotland. A very dear friend, Professor Jean-Charles Piette, or 'Monsieur Piette' as I privately think of him, was sending me a few words from the Isle of Skye. They began: 'A "stolen" week's holiday in Scotland.'

I must explain that this great clinical scientist, professor of internal medicine at the Hôpital de La Pitié and greatly loved by his patients, of whom I have been one for thirty years, lives only for them and his work. I have never known him not to be on the verge of physical and mental exhaustion, devoting hours to each patient, a doctor who is capable of accompanying the day's last home if he or she has been kept waiting too long, or of going to meet another patient's train (as he once did for me), who is capable of mad generosity and equally mad whims. And here he was, talking about a 'stolen' week. It leapt to the eye. Who was stealing what? Was he stealing a little respite from a world to which he owed all he could do, or was he not, instead, letting his all-consuming circle of acquaintances, his obsession with his work, his many and overwhelming responsibilities deprive him of his life? *We* are stealing his life from him, I thought, he is stealing his own life from himself.

So I began replying to him along these lines: every day you are missing out on what goes to make up the sweetness of life. And what does it do for you, apart from making you feel guilty for never doing enough? I began by setting down some major trails to follow, and soon entered into the spirit of the thing, seriously wondering what is, has been and will, I am sure, continue to be the sweetness of my own life.

So what follows here is an enumeration, an ordinary list in one long sentence, of ideas that came to me of their own accord by fits and starts, like a long, whispered monologue. It is about sensations, perceptions, emotions, minor pleasures and major joys, sometimes profound disillusionment and even pain, although my mind dwells more readily on the luminous than the sombre moments in life (and there have been some of the latter). Beginning with small and very general things that we must all have felt very real to us at some time or other, I have progressively drawn on private, lasting memories fixed for ever in powerful mental images, dazzling snapshots of experience that can, I think, be conveyed in a few words. This essay should be seen as a kind of prose poem paying tribute to life.

It is true that I think I have not had too many

problems in life. I have been lucky enough to deal, in my work, with intellectual questions that give depth and a singular touch of pleasure to everyday existence. I have enjoyed my work, and still do. I have also been lucky enough not to know poverty or, unlike millions of human beings today, enormous difficulty in simply surviving. What I have written here could therefore look like the hedonism of a woman who has led a privileged life. However, I will venture to think that, in describing pure sensuality, it evokes the actual experience of humanity in general.

The reader will become aware of the length of time involved. I was born before the Second World War, which made a great impression on me, although it did not entail much suffering on my own part. Indeed, it meant that during long holidays in this part of Auvergne that is now the Livradois National Park I became familiar with country life of a kind that is now in the past. I shall touch only lightly on the time I have spent in Africa and on my experience of illness. But many encounters will be found here, oddities, an attentive eye for nature and what it creates, for animals, noise, sounds, light and shade, aromas … and above all, other people.

The reader will not find glimpses of my private life in this essay, or very few of them. Nor will I dwell on the pleasures of the intellect, of research and writing, although those pleasures are intense. Or on love, although nonetheless it has played an important part in my life, as I suppose it will have done in those of readers. That was not my subject. What is it, then?

There is a kind of lightness and grace in the simple fact of existence, leaving aside our occupations, strong feelings, political and other commitments, and I wanted to confine my subject in this essay to that aspect. To the little plus factors that are granted to us all, and go to make up the flavour of life.

I was delighted to get your postcard yesterday
and know that you were taking a holiday in that
lovely place, an island to make anyone dream.
You sounded happy in the mists of Scotland. All
the same, you didn't 'steal' your holiday in the
sense of pilfering or misappropriating property.
Instead, I would say that you are stealing from
your own life every day.

If you assume an average life expectation of
85 years, or 31,025 days, always having, also on
average, 8 hours of sleep a day; if you spend 3
hours 30 minutes on shopping, preparing and
eating meals, washing up after them, and so
on; 1 hour 30 minutes on personal hygiene and
grooming, sickness, etc.; 3 hours on keeping the
family going: children, transport, interaction
with other people, DIY work, etc.; 140 hours of
work a month for 45 years at a rate of 6 hours
a day, leaving out of account the pleasure that
work may give you; 1 hour a day for obligatory
social relationships, conversations with the
neighbours, having a drink, meetings, seminars,
and so on; then how much time is left for the

average citizen, male or female, to enjoy those activities that are the sweetness of life?

Going on holiday, to the theatre, the cinema, the opera, concerts, exhibitions, reading, listening to music or playing it, various ways of taking exercise, walking, going on excursions, travel, gardening, visits to friends, relaxing, writing, creative arts, dreaming, reflection, sports (all of them), board games and party games, in fact games of any kind, doing crossword puzzles, resting, conversation, friendship, flirtation, love, and why not add guilty pleasures as well? You'll notice that I haven't even mentioned sex. You'll never guess: in what we think of as the active or working period of our lives, you have 1 hour 30 minutes a day for all that, and between 5 and 7 hours after, because the time returned to the other tasks increases.

And there you go extending your working hours by taking time from everything else, and missing out on all those pleasant things to which our deepest selves aspire.

I left out a lot of things in my list of those that make up the sweetness of life. So I will go on, following the method of the Surrealists, by looking at associations of ideas and letting them come of their own accord. All this may strike you as hedonistic, since I have left out all the subtleties of intellectual pleasure, or what we feel in commitments – and you may not even think it very serious if I'm not going to mention sex. Nonetheless, some things are very serious and very necessary if we are to preserve our 'zest' for life; I'm talking about the intimate thrill of small pleasures, I'm talking about questions and even setbacks if we give them time to exist. I will go on.

… I forgot about wild laughter, phone calls made for no real reason, handwritten letters, family meals (well, some of them), meals with friends, a beer at the bar, a glass of red or white wine, coffee in the sun, a siesta in the shade, eating oysters at the seaside or cherries straight from the tree, putting on a great show of anger, but only in pretence, making a collection (of

stones, butterflies, boxes or cans, how would
I know exactly what?), the bliss of fresh autumn
evenings, sunsets, waking up at night when
everyone's asleep, trying to remember the
words of old songs, searching for smells or
tastes, reading the newspaper in peace, looking
through photograph albums, playing with
a cat, building an imaginary house, setting
a place at table attractively, drawing casually
on a cigarette, keeping a diary, dancing (ah,
dancing!), going out to parties, going to the ball
on National Day, listening to the New Year
concert like millions of others, lounging on
a sofa, strolling along the streets and window-
gazing, trying on shoes, clowning around and
doing imitations, setting out to explore a city
you don't know, playing football or Scrabble or
dominoes, devising puns and plays on words,
talking nonsense, cooking a complicated dish,
going angling or jogging or playing bowls,
thinking all around an idea, watching an old
film on TV or in an experimental art-house
cinema, whistling with your hands in your
pockets, keeping your mind vacant, moments
of silence and solitude, running in warm rain,

long conversations at twilight, kisses on the back of the neck, the smell of warm croissants in the street, winks of complicity, the moment when all nature falls silent ... listening to the happy cries of children at play, feasting on ice cream or chocolates, those moments when you know that someone likes you, is looking at you and listening to you, feeling agile and sprightly, lying in late in the morning, getting on board a fishing boat, watching a craftsman at work, stopping to listen to a smooth talker peddling his wares (my goodness, that was a long time ago!), enjoying the sight of street life, getting back together with friends you haven't seen for ages, really listening to other people ...

And there's still so much else that I forget.

What about you, what would you miss most if all this had to disappear from your life for ever?

I can tell that I risk boring you to tears.

   ... listening with fanatical enthusiasm to Mozart, the Beatles, Astrud Gilberto, going on a trip to Switzerland and back in a single night to be at a concert given by your favourite singer, gorging on Alpine strawberries, walking on coastal roads on a windy day, waiting up to see an eclipse or eagle owl flying by night, racking your brains to think what would please someone you love, walking barefoot, listening to voices echoing over the sea, stretching and yawning, switching on either just a small flashlight or large projectors, paying compliments when you're going out for a good time, catching glances that say a great deal, turning down the corner of a page even though that's not the proper thing to do, throwing politeness out of the window for a while, forgetting to pick up your post, walking arm in arm or hand in hand with someone, going against the tide, holding the door open for an elegant old gentleman, curling up in a ball, breathing in the fresh air of early morning, watching branches shaken by the

wind, lighting a crackling fire, stuffing yourself
with sausage and pickled gherkins, waiting for
the moment when an angel briefly passes by (at
twenty minutes past, twenty minutes to, and on
the hour), putting your foot in it in company,
shaking your hair all over the place, smiling
at someone who's not expecting it, talking
seriously about a frivolous subject and joking
about a serious one (but mind who you do it
with!), not letting any louts or know-alls take you
in, enjoying what you like without inhibitions
(including the roar of racing cars), listening to
the life in your own body, sleeping flat on your
back, waving like Columbo, going upstairs four
steps at a time, arriving somewhere out of breath,
crying in the cinema, letting your emotions all
hang out or alternatively preserving an Olympian
calm, keeping quiet or admiring or listening,
taking cycling or playing the piano or archery
up again … using the luxurious restrooms of
a grand hotel while out walking, sitting down
in an armchair too deep for you, picking up
incongruous little items, plunging your hands
in the moss of a woodland floor or the foam of
detergent, listening to the local policeman's drum

roll (although they don't beat the drum these days) or barrel organs in the street (you don't get those either these days), racing your lover, sitting by an open window, waking up in a place you don't recognize, feeling your heart beat fast, weighing up arguments, testing the weight of a melon, seeing a childhood friend again, digging up buried memories (my God, yes, that's how it was!), taking your time over choosing some small thing (and deciding on important things in haste), following the flight of a single swallow among a flock of others, watching a cat from above when it doesn't know you're watching it, laughing up your sleeve, waiting for the twilight hour, watering your plants and talking to them, appreciating the touch of fine leather or a peach or someone's hair, studying the background of the *Mona Lisa* or the filigree effects of Vlaminck in detail, feeling pleasure at the sound of a voice, setting off for wherever the fancy takes you, staying in the dusk and doing nothing, cautiously trying grilled locusts, indulging in endless conversations with women friends of many years' standing, making up good stories ...

I'll go on, at the risk of boring you, because all
this is going to get more and more focussed. I get
the impression that I'm undermining banks
already on the point of collapse. After all,
I'm giving you ammunition for the day when,
in twenty years' time, people ask you what
I was like.

   … whispering on the telephone, fixing dates
years in advance, swooning over the bearing of
Robert Mitchum, the way Henry Fonda walks,
the smile of Brad Pitt, the romantic beauty
of Gene Tierney and Michelle Pfeiffer, the
ingenuous nature of Marilyn Monroe, the grace
of Audrey Hepburn; enjoying a *coppo del nonno*
coffee gelato in Florence, sighing with pleasure,
walking round a big department store, driving
on potholed tracks in a jeep, eating with your
fingers while crouching on the ground round
the dish, sharing a cola nut or chocolate bar,
being scared in the cinema, reading thrillers or
good SF, shamelessly taking the best peach out
of the fruit bowl, carefully extracting winkles
from their shells, eating in a real transport café

with a check tablecloth, making crystal glasses
ring, watching a good rugby match, playing
belote or rummy or the yam game or Ludo or
dominoes, being a bad sport among other bad
sports, protesting vehemently over nothing to
speak of, refusing to argue with angry people
(children included, and allowing yourself
the luxury of glaring at them in shops), also
allowing yourself the luxury of taxis reserved
in advance and looking at the queues outside
railway stations (*suave mari magno* …), having
an umbrella when you need one, a big enough
umbrella for several people, walking fast,
trailing your feet through dead leaves, smiling
lovingly at your grandmother's photograph,
listening to owls by night and crickets by
day, picking a bunch of wild flowers from
embankments, watching swathes of mist drift
by, following the course of a hare racing over
the fields or of Jean-Louis Trintignant round
the port of Nice in the film set there, trying to
pin down the moment when you fall asleep,
feeling the weight of your exhausted body in
bed, sleeping on someone's shoulder, joining
in a public festival, watching a good firework

display, listening to Callas singing or the wind moaning or hail pattering down, watching the fire, eating a sandwich in the street, walking on hot sand (but not too hot), sipping a drink, playing with a bunch of keys, urinating out of doors, being moved to tears, shouting for joy when you see a perfect shot at goal in football, caressing, being caressed, kissing, being kissed, hugging, being hugged (with love, complicity, affection), feeling full of drive, enthusiasm, passion, feeling your heart leap, ignoring conventions, admiring the young, having eyes bigger than your stomach, being deliciously scared, feeling unwell and opening your eyes to see friendly faces, enjoying an idea or a project or a memory by yourself, going out on the tarmac in Niamey in the rainy season and smelling the warm, spicy odour of African soil, seeing a pair of lions silently cross the trail in moonlight, taking an animal by surprise when its eyes are transfixed in a vehicle's headlights, talking all night, wanting to be surrounded by happiness, clearing out your cupboards, feeling surprised that you are still alive, being delighted when you suddenly find, in a flash, the solution to a problem that has been bothering you for ages, getting a present you like or a token of friendship or a postcard, singing popular songs in chorus, keeping secrets, conscientiously thinking up ideas, enjoying mild weather ...

And there's more to come …

… melting over the devastating restraint of Robert Redford in *Out of Africa* and the equally devastating insolence of Clark Gable in *Gone with the Wind*; sorting lentils, taking a pebble out of your shoe, having a bath at midnight, seeing the Northern Lights, turning somersaults and cartwheels in the grass (that was a long time ago!), finding a four-leaved clover, getting a game of patience to come out, rediscovering a taste for recipes of the past, calculating how many steps you take between stones on the pavements, listening to the little tune that tells you when a train is coming in or leaving, imagining what you could make of an object or a house or a place, choosing bread with a good crisp crust, picking grass to feed the rabbits, watering the flowers, knitting a soft scarf, seeing the curtain rise at the theatre when the lights go out and the noise of the audience dies down, just having time for a mouthful of a cocktail, crying while listening to *Die Winterreise*, going in search of the sources of rivers, paying a compliment to

a woman you don't know in the street, getting
the day, the week or the month wrong in
making a date, meeting again after twenty years
as if you'd never been parted, wearing a perfume
that makes you forget yourself, knowing how
to forget yourself, playing to the gallery, picking
up a child, protesting at his weight but not
bothering him with silly questions, wondering
where you were before you were born rather
than what happens to you after death, crumpling
up newspaper, cutting out pictures and making
collages, taking off or coming down in a plane,
looking enviously at dishes being served at the
next table in a restaurant, watching passers-by
and trying your hand at amateur psychology,
waiting outside a café, telling yourself you
ought to go to the gym, remembering to breathe
deeply now and then, starting to learn the
trombone from scratch, making mayonnaise or
beating egg whites for Îles flottantes by hand,
discovering a delicious exotic fruit, remembering
your baby language or proverbs or useful scraps
of knowledge, using surprisingly apt words,
drinking when you're very thirsty, never being
ashamed to be yourself …

… having an intimate conversation with
a Siamese cat or a Brittany spaniel, sneezing
seven times running, being first to spot the spire
of Trégunc church, having a picnic with all the
trappings, singing 'Stormy Weather' like Lena
Horne or 'Over the Rainbow' like Judy Garland,
trying to sing 'Mexico' like Luis Mariano and
failing to hit the high notes, losing yourself in
John Ford's vast skies, flying above the African
bush in a small aircraft, making stones bounce
as they skim the water, trembling with
impatience, feeling your taste buds react to
ginger, touching the moist nose of a calf, finding
mushrooms, picking wild bilberries, looking for
seashells at low tide, looking at your kitchen or
your bedroom or your office when you've
straightened it out, turning odd words over in
your mouth ('scullery', 'antiphon', 'mithridatic',
'hapax legomenon' …), riding on a cable-car
railway, jumping at the three blows announcing
the start of a performance in a French theatre,
playing hide and seek, winning a small
something in a raffle in the country, feeling

slightly scared in a long tree-lined avenue by
night, having a nice shower, getting your head
massaged, packing your cases, putting the key in
the lock, setting off on a journey, fishing for
crayfish with your bare hands (there are no more
of them), collecting edible snails (no more of
them either!), lying on a chaise longue, waiting
for the postman, shouting to hear the echo,
kicking a stone away, picking a scab on your
knee before the eyes of your disgusted parents
(that was all long ago!), having once got eighteen
out of twenty in maths, playing the harmonica
or the Jew's harp, having the last word, making
a wooden scale model, finishing a big jigsaw
puzzle, seeing Fujiyama or Kilimanjaro from far
away, wanting to go to Bobo-Dioulasso,
drinking in the words of someone you love,
watching James Stewart in a good western and
seeing the train winding its way over the plains
with a one-armed Spencer Tracy on board,
flinching with horror in your seat in front of
Alien or a zombie film, watching a tamarisk,
going to sleep while having magnetic resonance
imaging, cheering up the nurse who can't find
a vein, finding the young physician on duty

'irresistible', getting told off by a Swiss from Lausanne for crossing the road when the light is green but the little man is red, putting your hands in your pockets, jumping and bouncing on a bed (that was a long time ago too), taking an artichoke apart, spinning out a metaphor, finding good sunglasses, choking on a strong piri-piri pepper, giving a sharp reply if you have to, taming an animal, scanning the horizon in search of the island that you see only when it's going to rain, sweating blood over something you're writing and water when cycling uphill …

… going to a lot of trouble over nothing much, striking matches, polishing copper until it shines, dozing in a boring meeting, doing cryptic crossword puzzles, swearing like a trooper at things that keep getting in your way, not being taken in by pointed and flattering attentions, succumbing to greed, climbing the towers of Notre-Dame and dreaming of going to Machu Picchu, feeling the spray of Niagara Falls blown sideways into your face, walking all round an enormous baobab tree, drawing water from a well by the strength of your arms alone, without a pulley, enjoying the protection of a mosquito net, opening a gift package (what can be in it?), admiring a large Poitou donkey or Salers cow, throwing yourself on your bed in exhaustion with a sense of duty done, finishing a major washing-up session, climbing mountains in misty weather, in fine weather and in a cold wind, opening the bonnet of a car with steam coming out of it in the high mountain pass Casse Déserte de l'Izoard (this was on the verge of the 1950s), finding an old box of treasures with a fine

18

piece of mica in it, being aware of the transience of things and the necessity of seizing your chance, reciting a La Fontaine fable with feeling, overcoming idleness and fear of change, drinking a beer on a terrace late on a fine afternoon, shivering slightly as evening comes on, being impervious to the treacherous nature of some propositions, passing unnoticed when those who rule the roost are raking money in, failing to admire Mr Muscles and his biceps, leading a goat by its horns, being sworn at by a jealous Siamese cat, identifying instruments when you don't know what they are for, keeping quiet and speaking only after careful consideration, not feeling obliged to do the same as everyone else, wondering if the monastic life would be worth trying, being curious about everything, keeping your eyes open, happily breathing in the smell of new-mown hay or kelp, not so sure about the smell of mud at low tide, fording a river or crossing it on stepping stones, drawing a moustache on the *Mona Lisa* (and laughing secretly when you remember Marcel Duchamp's surrealist version of her), keeping so quiet that you deceive a bird, catching a fly in

one hand like Obama, hearing the cascading of
a waterfall, screaming blue murder when you sit
down in a car heated by the sun ...

… getting a guineafowl or any other creature as
a present still alive and kicking, having plenty of
boxes, lofts and roomy wardrobes, standing on
the edge of a sheer drop, imitating the voices,
movements and intonations of people or animals
to perfection, going to bed in sheets that have
just been changed, sanctimoniously contemplating
bucolic frescos, doing your nails, getting up and
saying no, putting your heart into a piece of
work, laughing with Coluche and Desproges,
Chaplin and Keaton, standing lost in baffled
thought in front of certain 'works of art', utterly
refusing to have certain books on your shelves
(for instance any by xenophobic writers and
Holocaust deniers), feeling at ease, even if
fleetingly, in body and mind … finding
a substitute for a flawed tool, reciting the list of
all the French departments and their capitals
(am not so sure of some of them!), laughing your
head off at female fashions of the 1930s but
liking those of ancient Crete, seeing the first
irises come into bloom, lovingly cutting cosmos
flowers for the house, raking up dead leaves,

bringing in the hay, appreciating the quality of silence after an orgy of sound, feeling surprised and moved by evidence of the past, beginning to read the newspaper at the back page, laughing at the crazy consequences of confusing right and left when reading a map, going out in the car before or after everyone else, or driving against the main flow of traffic and enjoying the illusion of being all-powerful, boiling an egg in an enormous pan (like Keaton), refraining for once from coming up with a witty retort only after the event ...

Is that the end?

… making a blade of grass between your
fingers and your lips whistle, listening in bed
at night to the Westminster chimes extending
their *ritornello* every quarter of an hour in the
kitchen at Bodélio, hearing the sound buoy
of Moelan 'moo', seeing a great stampede in
a western, stroking the soft, faded skin of an
old lady's hands, calling your mother 'my little
mother', your daughter 'my treasure', your
husband 'my heart' and feeling to the full
how accurate those descriptions are, dining in
a restaurant in an inner courtyard in a country
town, enjoying a funny rabbinical joke, singing
'Quand on s'promène au bord de l'eau' along with
Jean Gabin, knowing how to pronounce the
name of the town of Cunlhat properly, opening
a letter with your heart racing, being out of
doors when the devil marries his daughters
(what? Oh, sorry, meaning out in a shower
on an otherwise fine day), foretelling that it
will rain tomorrow from the angle of the rays
of the setting sun, solemnly calling a teenage

boy Monsieur, listening to the sweet voice of
Rina Ketty singing '*J'attendrai*' as she waits for
her man to come back and the piquant voice
of Mireille Mathieu in her song about *ce petit
chemin*; skipping around with Charles Trenet
and, with Yves Montand, looking at the legs of
the girl on a swing; for the first time and with
some inner trepidation using the Christian
name of someone you revere and who has
expressed a wish to be on first-name terms with
you, waking up in Paris to the music of Jacques
Dutronc, conscientiously licking the plate
clean, sitting in the sun in the Piazza Navona
in Rome in February while you eat a rocket
salad and drink a glass of Orvieto, holding
buttercups under your chin to see if there's
a yellow reflection, eating grapes straight from
the trellis on the front of a house, seeing large
raindrops splash down on the ground, or a huge
rainbow, or a distant light in the dark night
sky, or a shooting star or, very high up, a space
capsule silently passing; having a piggy bank,
a talisman, a slender waist, surprising an animal
going about its own business, feeling the density
of an attentive silence, entering a conversation

as you might enter the arena, finding the
right word for something at last, waiting for
a phone call, feeling sorry that pebbles lose
their beautiful colours as they dry, entertaining
the fantasy of a big house with green shutters
standing at a crossroads in the heart of a forest,
admiring the entrance of a house reached
by two elegant flights of steps, or opulent
hollyhocks or a porch roofed with glazed tiles,
singing a cappella and in unison, vibrating at
the sound of a voice, being struck directly by
troubling likenesses and acting with a newcomer
as you would with an old acquaintance, talking
to yourself in private, loyally retaining a certain
idea of those you have loved, getting the proofs
of a new book, eating wild honey from combs
gathered by smoking the bees out, crunching
radishes, making apple compote and shortcrust
pastry tarts, drinking fresh cider, sleeping out
of doors, admiring the nocturnal labours of
termites under shoes left on the floor of a hut,
drinking warm millet beer from a calabash and
passing it to your neighbour, going for a long
drive along a rough track without puncturing
a tyre; seeing the white coat of the medical

supervisor you are waiting for in his hospital
department at the end of the corridor, as he
stalks along like a tall heron in a hurry, and
feeling comforted, full of joy and well-being;
loving of all the life during field-work, even in
discomfort, striking up a conversation easily,
coming to terms with what you hate, herding
cows, drawing wine from a cask, watching
the fingertips of your doctor's expert hands
as they identify what's wrong, artlessly saying
something funny and paying attention only
to your audience's laughter, going all the way
down a long steep street in a car without
stopping at the crossroads some day, going to the
hairdresser's, having a manicure …

This is addictive. I'll go on.

   … keeping perfectly still in front of a black
mamba that has not woken up properly, loving
House and the Goth girl with black bunches
in *NCIS* and the character of Ally McBeal,
skipping a rope held by two girlfriends turning
it faster and faster (that was back in prehistory),
enjoying a gin fizz with the rim of the glass
frosted or a Campari and soda, eating pistachio
and cashew nuts one after another, dipping
a sugar lump in your neighbour's coffee cup,
scraping up the sugary residue from the bottom
of the cup, surviving the attack of a swarm of
wild bees in the African bush, breathing in
the powerful odour of hot tar or the faintly
nauseating smell of the manufacturing of shea
butter, swerving athletically to avoid ruts too
deep for your tyres, imagining the underside of
crinoline dresses, listing all sorts of loincloths
for men, managing to haul yourself back
into a hospital bed on your own, knowing
that the man you are waiting for will come,
seeing the landscape opening out like a corolla

from the top of a hill, feeling the earth turn
beneath your feet while you watch the clouds
… calculating the time between lightning and
thunder, scrutinizing the darkness and seeing
strange snaky shapes like lamias there, making
people think you can read the future in coffee
grounds, trying to get a game of cards to work
out, coming back in triumph from a cookery
class one day, after learning to make celery
rémoulade, and stuffing the family with it
for days; remembering the shame of faux pas
committed in the past, going to midnight mass
at the church of St Augustin and sliding along
the rue du Général Foy, its frozen surface still
wooden at the time; having been very good at
putting the shot and no other kind of sport at
all; trying to work out what deserved a great
historian's congratulations before realizing
that he was talking about himself; wearing
a pretty red dress to the wedding of a friend,
the son of an ambassador to the USSR (that
dates me), to a novelist who was already famous;
cycling fast up slopes like Gino Bartali in the
Tour de France but braking hard on the way
down; laughing in a bumper car although you

hated it, going on the dance floor with only
an accordionist and a drummer, waltzing
wonderfully well but also liking to dance the
java, the rumba, the paso doble, the tango,
even rock (yes, I did!), sitting up all night to
finish reading a novel, sitting up all night with
the first death in my family (of the mother of
my mother's mother), sitting up all night with
a baby, hearing a little tune by Mozart that
always makes the heart turn over, falling off
a platform in front of a hundred people, getting
up and going on as if nothing had happened,
playing the 'What if?' game; paddling in the
sea, touching sensitive plants, carefully picking
cactus fruits, stroking a tame hedgehog, having
a pet sheep called Pedro, watching the cat Petite
Demoiselle fight a rat in a granary (the cat won),
eating on one and the same day in Livradois
warm rye bread cut up in a tart, potatoes 'for
the pigs' cooked in a big pan, freshly churned
butter and cake with black cherries (this was
in the war, and it could have been yesterday),
remembering the wartime radio programme *Ici
Londres* and seeing the maquisard Resistance
fighters in Auvergne, sheltering in cellars

during air raids on Saint-Étienne, Firminy, La
Ricamarie, Rive-de-Gier, loving the brownish
sugar that melted in compote dishes and potato
cakes (a thick, filling dish), watching the great
meeting of the political Left at the gates of
Versailles with François Mitterrand, Georges
Marchais and Robert Fabre, hearing the news
of the French May 1968 protests when I was
in the bush over a crackling transistor radio
brought by an immigrant from Ghana; reacting
violently to the opulence of our shopping streets
on my return from ascetic periods in Africa,
attending several meetings of the emergent
Movement for the Liberation of Women (MLF)
near Montsouris Park; keeping everything
I have been given, helpfully giving information
to tourists and people who had lost their way so
that I was late myself; writing by hand, being
obsessed for a while with an encounter yet to
come or the precise point of an argument yet to
be settled or the best way of setting out an idea;
making tea, organizing an impromptu dinner,
returning to consciousness in a reanimation
room after being in a coma and thinking briefly
that this was the end of me; being happy when

your child is happy, soaking up feelings, feeling
everything strongly but not letting it show …
having no more toothache (or any other kind
of ache), making a door or a step on the stairs
or chalk on a slate squeal, picturing everything
very clearly in the imagination, treasuring the
ugly photo of my mother in a cycling jersey
posing beside her bike for the local paper at
the age of over sixty after an amateur cycle
race, feeling incapable of such an achievement,
always doubting my own abilities and worrying
about the veracity of praise that I have received
(how well trained in modesty we were!);
knowing my star sign as Scorpio with Cancer
in the ascendant and reading horoscopes with
amusement; getting annoyed with the titles
that newspapers impose on interviews or on
articles you send them, feeling satisfaction at
hoarding two-euro coins away in a box so as
not to be caught without cash; retaining ever
since the days of rationing a terror of going
short, worrying about running out of petrol and
still having to find the hotel before nightfall,
particularly with children in the car; waiting
for my daughter outside school or making her

a snack to take, exchanging letters with her
containing clumsy drawings by both parties,
playing at Sleeping Beauty with her, laughing
at ads claiming 'I wouldn't do this every day',
finding myself unable to remember funny
stories, trusting my brother and never getting
bored by him; avoiding weightiness without
giving up your own point of view, hating a curt
tone of voice, stiff, coarse, offensive manners,
disdainful looks, the lack of consideration for
others that you find in those who, for some
reason, think themselves superior; always
talking and acting in the same way, in the
same tone of voice and the same language, in
front of everyone; considering that the word
'kindness' denotes a great virtue, not looking
away from adversity, regarding friendship as
a commitment, getting absorbed in watching
an anthill at work, walking into a field to
make the grasshoppers leap out, knowing
where red squirrels nest, having large keys to
the barred gates in your garden, letting weeds
grow between the paving stones of a terrace,
being unable to do without nasturtiums in
the garden, making a ladybird walk on your

finger, watching milk on the stove and taking it off the heat just in time, making a chocolate mousse to my mother's old recipe (with butter in it), still feeling nostalgic about poached eggs in red wine sauce, being naively astonished by conjuring tricks, being dazzled by a fine sight and captivated by a good speech …

… being invited to the country by friends you are fond of and discovering that the ocean lies just beyond their house, and there's the priest's garden with its orchard and cottage-garden flowers; admiring your great-uncle's handsome moustache in the Vercingetorix style and your old cousin's grating voice (the result of being gassed in 1914), which resembles the voice of historian Henri-Irénée Marrou after tracheotomy; enjoying coffee (with milk for those who like it white) and sharing biscuits with your cousin's dogs and cats who sit like good children around the big table; stretching out at length with your hands behind your head and your feet on the coffee table (sad to say I can't prop mine on a desk as characters do in old American films), hoping to succeed in striking a match on the sole of your shoe some day or hold a revolver, metaphorically speaking, like Humphrey Bogart, watching *Butch Cassidy and the Sundance Kid* again, also *Kiss Me Deadly*, *The Incredible Shrinking Man*, *A High Wind in Jamaica* and *The Dead*; remembering listening conscientiously to the daily 5 p.m. reading from

Molly Bloom's monologue on Europe 1 (which could almost be called a cultural radio channel in its early stages); having a horror of deadlines, leafing through catalogues like those of the Manufrance mail-order firm (I was told that at the age of three I meticulously studied every picture as I turned its pages), inhaling the smell of a book little by little before beginning to reread it from the first to the last line, provided that it made a good first impression, discovering new words (one of mine is the slightly suspect but marvellous 'procrastination', picked up rather late in life!), shedding tears in front of the TV set when the cheetah in the animal documentary discovers his mortally wounded brother and prowls around him, scolding him, while the wounded creature follows him with his eyes, groaning like a human child … waiting for the moment in the film *The Bear* when the bear draws himself up to his full height in front of Tchéky Karyo, playing the part of the hunter, who is paralysed by fear and humility; being surprised to find Leonardo DiCaprio playing a simple-minded adolescent with a nervous laugh who dreams only of climbing to the top of

the water tower, and Robert De Niro talking to
himself in his little room ('you talkin' to me?');
coming out of the Métro on an empty platform,
running through a heavy thunderstorm and
taking refuge, laughing, under an awning;
tasting salty caramel; going through a forest or
a huge park full of balanzan trees, or a desert, or
salt marshes or mangrove swamps or the
Dombes region near Lyon, wondering about the
shape or colour of an artichoke flower or
a eucalyptus seed, trying to imagine the long
journey taken by the voice that reaches you all
the way from Sydney; fuming with impatience
as things pile up to make you late (staying in bed
too long, no taxi, traffic congestion …); watching
the work of an itinerant farrier, seeing donkeys
and goats pass by with their little bells on their
way back from the Jardin du Luxembourg, or
the Republican Guard on horseback, or
a procession of vintage cars all going out on
a country road; picking mulberries, escaping an
angry bull or a discontented goose or
a watchdog, watching with annoyance as the
tongues of interested cows snap up the fine
mushrooms you were going to pick, blushing

and being cross with yourself for it, loving someone who has no idea of it … sharing your plate in a restaurant, ordering a dish at random when you're abroad, polishing up an old wardrobe, never tiring of listening to Miles Davis or Thelonious Monk, putting a misogynist in his place by using his own range of expressions, pouring orange-flower water into your maternal grandmother's glass out of pure kindness, only to find her surprised later by the strange flavour of the wine: 'I assure you, Étienne (her son-in-law), this wine is truly undrinkable!', being surprised to find yourself connected, during a phone call, to a conversation with strangers, listening to your grandmothers talk family matters at length, marvelling at pictures by Hokusai or calligraphy or Portuguese *azulejos* tiles or grass skirts, having a basket full of African bracelets …

… dreading an untimely scarlet stain on your white trousers, avoiding any such danger and going home in good time, drinking from the bottle or without letting your lips touch its rim, placing a round loaf upside down and remembering ancestral reproaches: 'That's no way to earn your bread' (i.e. lying idle on your back), arranging fruit in a basket, being in a car with tinted windows so that you can't be seen from outside, opening a bottle with a wine stock and making the cork vibrate with a 'plop', collecting glow-worms, catching the scent of your grandmother's eau de cologne in the street, admiring the dresses worn by the heroine of the fairy-tale musical film *Peau d'Âne*, dreaming of having the long, slender legs and melancholy look of Italian madonnas with the baby Jesus on their knees or the artistic blonde pallor of Tilda Swinton, feeling I wanted to die on the spot the day – long ago now – when Claude Lévi-Strauss asked out of the blue if I had any comment to make after a lecture by someone else that I had not understood and promising myself never to

put anyone else in the same position, carefully
choosing a bracelet for a woman friend,
comforting a soul in pain, being given marrons
glacés, to have seen Cocteau's *The Eagle Has Two
Heads* at the Théâtre Hébertot with Edwige
Feuillère and Jean Marais, who could have
looked ridiculous but didn't in leather trousers
with braces, picking daffodils once in a forest
near Paris, being close one day to the strong
odour of a real billy goat, spending hours
studying the two classic chromolithographs of
the Ages of Life, to have been captivated by the
beauty of my father's large, flexible hands;
inhaling at length, with eyes closed, the secret
aroma of tar and the sea in the hair of a beloved
person who allows you to do so, drawing a pretty
blue line at the corners of your eyes; being taken
by surprise when a girl said, with tears in her
eyes, how moved she is to meet you, trying to
surprise a snail by touching its feelers,
inadvertently giving yourself an electric shock in
the elbow, admiring the fine looks of a group of
adolescent girls, falling into ecstasies over the
colour and transient form of a hibiscus flower,
considering that because of our fixed ideas of the

number forty you are older at forty than at fifty or sixty, worrying, being afraid of committing a faux pas or of a delay or of what people will say, attracting the attention of someone whose approval you want, being ridiculously pleased with what you have just done ...

… never to have read certain great writers but
remembering with delight the mysterious word
'*morne*' that I found in the West Indies of my
first real children's book, spending two months
in a boarding school for deaf-mutes while my
brother was suffering from scarlet fever, enjoying
solitude and avoiding too effervescent an
atmosphere, seeing likenesses without ever being
able to draw, reviving the dead by talking about
them, excoriating yourself mentally for
cowardice, laziness, vacillation and uncertainty,
lack of a sense of coherence, susceptibility,
slowness, greed, a propensity for putting things
off until tomorrow, fear of disturbing other
people and many more faults, coming upon the
adjective 'suspicious' used by a friend to explain
why his emotional experiences ended badly,
which made me wonder how anyone can live
without trust; feeling at times, when pain went
away, a sense of absolute happiness that goes to
the heart and almost hurts; knowing someone so
indifferent to everyday life that he has to look
out of the window if he is asked on the phone if

it is fine or raining, mentally adopting my
grandmother's unsparing judgements and pithy
epithets: a stuck-up female, a total idiot,
a halfwit, a gossip, a bragger, a belligerent,
a fatso, a virago, a clumsy clot, someone always
trying to piss higher than last time, a happy
imbecile, a hussy, the wrong sort, an old dragon,
a great goof, a pain in the neck, a real tart, a bad
penny, a proper little madam, a down-and-out,
someone who knocks around, all of which bears
witness to her moral ideas and her conception of
'gender'! … also being up in arms, figuratively
speaking, when an adult puts you in the same
category as his grandparents – oh, and what else
is there? … being glad to have few wrinkles but
bothered by ugly scars; admiring newborn
babies, their tiny hands, their round eyes, their
perfectly formed mouths, all those parts into
which knowledge and love will pass; going to
the Easter lamb and kid fair sometimes, liking
the market, the fresh eyes of a fish, the mounds
of fruit, great blocks of Cantal cheese, the herb
stall; listing with delight the wealth of hardware
and haberdashery and trimmings available,
trembling with joy at the idea of giving someone

a nice surprise, telling stories, reading aloud;
loving four cats at various times: Roulette,
a timid cat from the Auvergne with grey fur;
Julie, a demanding and voluble blue-point
Siamese; Petite Mère, a knowing tabby from
Brittany, and her son Mitchum, a sweet, paler
tabby with a handsome chest; never having
managed to satisfy the appetite of a greedy
nanny goat called Aglae, not even with forty-
eight apple turnovers, pains au chocolat with
raisins, palmier biscuits and brioches; and as
a child (together with my sister and our girl
cousin) getting an old and very rustic nanny goat
drunk on rum-cream dessert …

… collecting the full set of the *Cahiers du cinéma*, regretting that I don't look good in a hat, liking to wear first red and then black and now blue, sobbing in silence for hours looking at the human figures like 'black commas' falling from the Twin Towers on 11 September, loving old toys that get put away again, always searching (although in vain) for the real taste of Reinette apples from Le Mans, or stoned apricots tasting of honey, or vineyard peaches or gooseberries, uninhibitedly using words and expressions that are family inventions: the air here is very 'soapoforic', don't cast 'nasturtiums' on him … giving up when faced with picture puzzles and guessing games, sometimes remaining naive and not minding; flying off the handle when someone said of Simone de Beauvoir's *The Second Sex* that it 'wasn't bad for a woman' and putting him in his insignificant place with a few well-chosen words; going down the great avenue in Bodélio park in the time of its splendour before the great storm struck, once knowing a cat who vociferously demanded to be let out

when a little girl took her violin out of its case
… laughing uproariously at my father imitating
the gorilla and then with fear at the opening
scene of Mario Bava's horror film *Black Sunday*,
suffering nightmares for ages because of
Radot's *The Wolf of the Malveneurs*; being able to
laugh my head off or weeping my eyes out
simply by thinking of something, feeling
serenely at home in the internal medicine
department of La Pitié hospital, having had my
wrists tied when I had chickenpox so as not to
scratch myself, herding cows while making
rosaries, riding as a child on the back of the big
shepherd dog Bijou, hitting out at roosters which
to childish eyes were attacking harmless hens
when they jumped on them, regretting never
having seen a woman giving birth or indeed any
other creature, even my cat Julie kittening,
dining on excellent local charcuterie, then an
Auvergnat dish of bacon and all the vegetables,
then pigeons with peas, then a jugged hare
('I'm acquainted with that hare,' said the cousin
who had snared it), then roast veal from the local
butcher with small round potatoes fried in
walnut oil and big white Soissons haricot beans,

followed by salad, and then the house's goat cheese, and then pears in wine with biscuits and then an apple tart (phew!) with coffee and a glass of the local spirits, all extensively and lavishly garnished; emerging from a long period of ill health resembling a tornado and telling myself it must be fine outside, trying to pacify a woman who was disturbed and calling for the nurse all night; feeling carried away by a heavy, rhythmic swell at sea and forgetting that everything is finite, groping about in search of a flashlight (which didn't work), remembering, decades later, a simple organdie dress that felt scratchy, hesitating to put my hand under a stone after seeing *The Treasure of the Sierra Madre*, and casually throwing an envelope with my name and address on it in a waste bin in the street after reading Patricia Highsmith; thinking of the workings of chance that mean we are not contemporaries of people we would like to have known, telling yourself that a lion with a thorn in its paw or hedgehog spines in its nose must feel really handicapped, hearing your own voice over a loudspeaker, enjoying the atmosphere of the graveyards of little towns on All Saints' Day, seeing Frankenstein in person, otherwise known as the gravedigger, emerging from the graveyard; to have looked after litters of kittens and superfluous piglets who were suckled by a goat, remembering strolling along brilliant streets, wondering with concern what we would have done in circumstances that in fact we were spared … engaging in hopeless battles with the castors of trolleys and mobile drips, hating the resistance of inanimate objects; assessing the difference in perception of the past between your own memories and those of your brother and sister, husband, daughter, marvelling at the ability of the human species to adapt, seething inside at some people's cheerful stupidity or childishness or self-importance or cowardice or malice, refusing to speak provincial language, blushing at my pronunciation of English, imagining people's characters from their voices, pitying those stars of the silent screen who, like John Gilbert, had falsetto voices and whose careers therefore came to a sudden end, liking voices that are deep or hesitant or precise or warm or laughing or sweet or have a catch in them, and attributing a physique and a never-

changing age to each voice; relishing the sound
in your mouth of a sparkling word like
'ampersand' or the mischief of 'charivari' or the
grotesque 'rookie' for a soldier or the skittish
'Trastevere' or the emphasis of 'distinguished
salutations' or the nostalgic sound of 'souvenir'
… coming back from Italy in a convertible
yellow Fiat, rebelling against stupidity at the
right moment, opening shutters and windows
wide to let in currents of air, shivering with
a sense of having caught a chill, jumping at the
sound of doors slamming, seeing sheets put out
to dry blowing in the wind, admiring the
beautiful wisteria on certain houses, feeling
happy to find that everywhere, or almost
everywhere, the placid facades of our railway
stations are made to the same design, liking the
look of windmills, great birds that sometimes
threaten to injure birds of flesh and blood; being
fundamentally, radically, quietly happy to be of
my own sex but liking the opposite sex as well,
finding a nest of grey mice in the bed the day
after coming home from months of absence,
getting cross with the dormice ensconced above
the ceiling, watching impotently as crows attack

a tawny owl's nest, putting out dishes of fat and seeds for the birds in the trees in winter and finding them empty in spring, enduring the Harmattan trade wind of West Africa that dries your lips and burns your lungs, sharing the childish joy of being out in the first warm rains of June, seeing a Mercedes without wheels that is now a toy for the children of the Yatenga Naba, king of Waiguiyua, in a yard with mud walls in Burkina Faso, being palpated intimately at close quarters by the dry, intrusive hands of old ladies who came out of the bush to discover what sex this peculiar person was; wanting in the past to look like Simone Simon, being too short for my liking, being dismayed by the stupid opulence of the tall, disliking baths, fearing the results of having my hair cut at the hairdresser's unless Stéphanie does it, enjoying the epistolary novel in such titles as Mary Ann Shaffer and Annie Barrows' *The Guernsey Literary and Potato Peel Pie Society*, liking things that murmur, whisper, reach the ear like drops of crystal running down stalactites, living faithful to your own ideas, friends and loves, having moods of enthusiasm but also of uneasiness, eating a supper of

pig's ears after the theatre, hating the atmosphere
at the sales, trying to catch yourself snoring, being
transported by joy after winning a little victory
over the way to use my Apple Mac, discovering
that a driving licence was the most difficult and
thus the most gratifying certificate that I ever
gained, enjoying the company of women friends,
cherishing photographs and such small things
like the apple of my eye, eating a chocolate in two
mouthfuls as a reward for a great effort or
a victory, catching rainwater to rinse the hair,
enjoying running after the bus to catch it by
jumping on the back platform when the
conductor lifted the chain, planting a big kiss on
the nose of a cat who took offence, making
a date with someone I loved at the other end of
the world, but specifying just where very
precisely (and in six months' time) and then not
finding the place (which no longer existed), but
although mobiles were not yet in use finding it
all the same; keeping a list of everywhere you
happen to have slept on a journey, going away
with a companion at least once a month so that
the two of you can discover new places, trying
to follow a conversation in a foreign language in

which words of your own surface now and then, liking cave dwellings wherever they are, not really caring for the impersonal voices at airports, triumphantly going down the sunny side of the street in pink trousers one fine April morning, feeling sudden outbursts of joy as you might feel fits of heat, peeling *scorzonera* and finding they turn your fingers black, addressing yourself to a face you have picked out in an audience, being terribly afraid of being kept waiting for a long time by those you love, rolling up your sleeves in the real as well as the figurative sense, catching a ball in the air, candling eggs, peeling sweet chestnuts, relishing complicated family trees and remembering other people's as well as you remember your own, liking large puppets, being crazy for West Coast jazz and Bix Beiderbecke, the 'young man with a horn', getting lost in Saenredam's tall white churches with their high aisles and heavy doors, standing transfixed in front of the thick paste of Van Gogh's violet irises, to have dined at the famous three-star Troisgros restaurant when there really were three of the family running it, eating liquorice, eating millet porridge with

a sauce of fresh baobab leaves, finding a misprint
on the fourth reading of a proof, reading
accounts of snowstorms, sitting doing nothing,
hands dangling, looking into space, appreciating
the beauty of cranes on a building site at rest, of
industrial landscapes and disused railways, being
cross with myself for talking too fast or wanting
to finish sentences for people who speak slowly,
applauding the successful backward passes of the
wide line of attacking players racing forward at
a time when rugby really was an attacking
game, living for long periods in an African hut
made of the fermented mud called banco,
buying rustic plates in Cambridge market,
appreciating at its true value the venomous
hissing of Agnes Moorehead before she goes out
of the window in *Dark Passage*, seeing out of the
corner of an eye a small grey mouse scurrying
furtively into the kitchen in the country, tacking
in a felucca while sailing on the Nile and seeing
the work done on the project to rescue the
temples on the island of Philae; remembering
the ugliness of an enormous monkfish in the
port of Marettimo and of staying there as
a moment of grace, picturing Earth rushing

through space under your body lying flat in
a meadow covered with daisies, eating courgette-
flower fritters, and in childhood consuming
heart-shaped waffles made one by one in an
adjustable black waffle iron on the heat of
ancient cookers, holding back the tears at the
first words of my inaugural lecture, getting
Umberto Eco invited to the European Chair of
the College of France and thus, in front of
a large audience, forcing the minister responsible
to take note of the striking absence of lecture
rooms worthy of the name in that institution (we
do now have the Marguerite de Navarre lecture
hall); having seen Jean Vauthier's play *La
Nouvelle Mandragore* from the raised seats on
stage at the Théâtre de Chaillot and then
approaching the legendary Gérard Philipe;
watching the moon shine brightly in a sky full of
luminous clouds, remembering the great jazz
age days of the Café Tournon, of Richard
Wright, of Chester Himes (Coffin Ed and
Gravedigger Jones) and Slim, remembering the
post-war Christian Dior dresses with swirling
flared skirts and cinched waists; loving the films
of François Truffaut and the very individual

voice of Delphine Seyrig, to have travelled by
Caravelle airliner, stopping off three times on the
flight to Ouagadougou, waiting two years for
a phone line to be installed, remembering mail
sent by pneumatic tube, the death of a pope two
months after his election, the pleasure of
walking down the rue de la Huchette to go to
Maspero or the Caveau to listen to jazz, seeing
Miles Davis, all those anodyne things that have
become the mark of an era, loving words, the
feel of them in the mouth, their sonority, owning
large numbers of scarves that never get worn,
inheriting six crystal glasses, featuring as
a birthday present given by loving parents to
their daughter when I agreed to see her, having
my opinions strengthened by letters from
unknown admirers, spending hours in
conversation with Francis who is clever and
attentive; playing at the children's character of *la
petite bête qui monte qui monte* with my baby in
fits of laughter, seeing Corpus Christi processions
with sheets at the windows and baskets of rose
petals, remembering a cousin who milked her
cows by hand with a clothes peg on her nose,
seeing babies grow while old people shrink,

amusing myself by talking in alexandrines, relishing the 'sweetness of Anjou', living at one time above the Gare Montparnasse and feeling as if I were facing the transatlantic liner in *Amarcord* with all its portholes lit up, having big cuddles, amazement at the eroticism of the silent film *Queen Kelly* and the blazing eloquence of Daniel Day-Lewis in *The Age of Innocence*, enjoying the preciosity of David Suchet as Hercule Poirot as much as the rough and ready approach of Lino Ventura or the perversity of a sniggering Richard Widmark or the astonishing gentleness of Gene Tierney in *The Ghost and Mrs Muir*, melting at the awkward look of Henry Fonda when told to dance the waltz in the final ball of *My Darling Clementine* …

… enjoying the austere world of *Dune* and its subterranean cathedrals of water, visiting the Montsouris reservoir, trying to revive a thrush that killed itself colliding with a windowpane and seeing the distress of the bird's partner who came back to the scene several days running; tinkering with old furniture, repainting a large room with the help of friends and relations, feeling at ease in the delicate architecture of the Great Mosque of Cordoba, admiring the huge black-bull silhouettes along the roads of Spain, picking a bunch of foxgloves, being present, frozen and drenched, at the bicentenary celebrations of the Revolution on the platforms in the place de la Concorde where the wind blew water from the fountains over the guests, always feeling particularly moved by a tiny church standing on its green esplanade, declining to eat cucumbers with cream and chantilly cream in general, loving municipal brass bands and watching end-of-the-year school shows, meeting the handsome bullfighter Luis Miguel Dominguín in his glory days, seeing strong

minds weep at the death of Michel Foucault,
sleeping in prickly hay, being a spectator at the
full Christmas dinner given by the café
proprietor who was mayor of Bertignat and his
wife to a genuine vagabond wearing
a huntsman's pouch and laced boots, who asked
only for hot water and salt to cook his vermicelli
and a glass of wine (he got two), to have heard
some wonderful speakers, to have felt deeply
confused as I raised an old lady from her knees
while she begged me to make sure that her baby
grandchild was cared for after her daughter had
died in childbirth (I complied with her request)
… driving on African roads like corrugated iron
which were sure to ruin vehicles failing to reach
the requisite speed, and following the fine tracks
left by bicycle wheels tracing a zigzag course
around natural obstacles on dusty or lateritic
ground; feeling (mistakenly) sure of imminent
death, trying to write legibly, dreaming of an
attractive Yves Saint-Laurent pair of trousers for
evening wear or a wonderful dress seen in
a magazine, being astonished by the subject for
a thesis about the 'adhesive capacity of hairs on
the front legs of a Madagascar spider', swooning

at the sight of the lovesick King Kong but
wondering how on earth anyone ever got him
back into the ship's hold, spitting out grape or
orange or mandarin or watermelon seeds or
apple pips (we can forget about avocado stones),
getting to the heart of the subject, analysing
a complex theme with precision, adding the final
full stop to a text, seeing a deserted café standing
up to the weather on the road, remembering,
with a wry smile, having lessons in the social
graces at school at the age of twelve or thirteen,
almost drowning myself while laughing too
loudly, crashing into two stationary cars coming
out of a garage, remembering with emotion all
my returns to the field in Africa, learning to take
my bearings by the Pleiades, driving for hours
through the thorny African bush, seeing that
strange animal the aardvark, spending a whole
night dripping with water under a clay roof that
was dissolving in the rain, knowing some hidden
springs, recollecting with pleasure those few
encounters that have really made their mark on
me, rejoicing secretly when something turns out
exactly as foreseen, deciding that there's a touch
of chill in the air and it would be a good idea to

put on a jumper, marvelling at the way people
around you are getting younger whilst taking
lessons from a 25-year-old teacher of computer
technology, feeling moved by my
mother's dictum that she always felt twenty
inside herself, and by the failure of my own
father to recognize me, rediscovering the
macaroon smell of gorse every summer, going to
pick bilberries in the woods and coming back
with lips stained black, feeling pain gently slip
away when morphine takes effect, being crazy
about the Robert Graves works based on Greek
mythology, knowing that one way or another
I have always been at school, living sparingly at
the time of the Suez Crisis on a thin baguette
and a cup of coffee a day and, with gratitude,
dining one evening with a girlfriend's parents
who were diamond merchants, receiving
a proposal of marriage in Djerba from a local
Tunisian who was fascinated by high-necked
dresses, greeting the *hogon*, priest of the Dogon
people, outside the tall facade of his house with
its regularly spaced niches to hold animal skulls,
spending hours admiring the minute details of
relief maps of the cities of North Africa, going

on a cruise with a woman friend, riding
a dromedary on one occasion, liking Turkish
delight and honey pastries, listening to the calls
of crows in the Indian Museum in Ottawa,
laughing again at the memory of a kitten seen at
a roadside in Togo eating pieces of chilli-
flavoured meat voraciously but with its fur
bristling, remembering the swallows in the sky
of Paris and the funfair that went from Clichy to
Monceau, eating spice cake, succumbing to
a Belgian speculoos biscuit, going into a house
with the smell of cinnamon-flavoured apples in
the air …

… asking a group of three punks sporting Mohican hairstyles and Doc Martens the way one rainy winter evening at the deserted exit from the Censier-Daubenton Métro station as they fooled around in the shelter of a porch, and then being escorted by three considerate young men: 'Of course we're coming with you, you wouldn't have found the way by yourself, and you might need protection at this time of night …', driving at breakneck speed down the empty motorway to the west which had just been opened in a luxurious Facel-Vega lined with blond leather that smelled of honey, often adding wine to bacon soup in the country, eating rustic cheeses in the war when maggots leapt athletically out of them, their little bodies curving in the air, having stopped at Sully-sur-Loire during the exodus in 1940 to hand glasses of water with my big sister, then aged nine, to the soldiers taken prisoner who kept filing past (we were allowed to do it, adults were not), remembering my sixteenth birthday and a wide-skirted white dress with a pattern of large

green polka dots and a big collar, a later red
faille silk dress with a close-fitting top and
a flared skirt and two little white organdie wings
at the shoulders, also a short dress made of
openwork black lace, very close-fitting and with
a square neckline, and another dress, chestnut-
coloured velvet with a laced waistcoat in
a golden-brown herringbone fabric, a wide black
leather belt forming a corselet and a pair of
bright purple shoes with silver high heels for
dancing; always feeling slightly uneasy in front
of the depths of one of those large, heavy
Burgundian wardrobes lined with fabric with
a dark-green moiré effect, where you feel that if
you slipped into it you might be swallowed up by
the darkness or emerge into a bright light,
marvelling to hear, in your head, the voices of
several people now dead but not all of them, no,
and without knowing why you hear these voices
and not others; playing with your fingers, feeling
like a stone closed in on itself, and at moments
of intense fear, discomfort or emotion in your
life knocking at a tall wooden door with
a copper knocker; closing your eyes the better to
hear the sound of the wind in tall poplar trees

and feeling it blow on your face; hating hair
hanging in your eyes or wearing lipstick or
having scarves tied tightly round your neck, or
a handbag carried over your elbow, or wearing
flesh-coloured underclothes or anything fitting
so tightly that it cuts you under the arms;
making sure you are paid with a small coin
when giving someone a present of a knife or
a paperknife; enjoying witty remarks, a sense of
humour, even facetious comments or irony but
hating sarcasm; instinctively seeking out what is
unusual, incongruous, discordant; the light of all
that is strange that passes over like lightning, but
also graceful movements, pretty gestures,
a supple way of getting out of an armchair,
knowing that thinking makes time pass fast and
you will emerge disconcerted; liking Gloria
Grahame's pointed chin, her sparkling eyes and
her cascading laughter; fearing quicksands or
a mudslide, or feeling your foot turn over or
falling flat on your back on the tall, narrow steps
of the Mexican pyramids; making lavish bunches
of hydrangeas; replying with a smile to the silent
question asked by all small babies: 'Who on
earth are you?'

*

As you can see, my dear friend, we're
not talking about high-flown metaphysical
speculation, or profound reflections on the
vanity of existence, or the passionate private life
of everyone on earth. We are simply concerned
with the way to make everything in life
a treasure of grace and beauty that always keeps
growing of its own accord, in a place where you
can draw on it daily. There's no real magic in
any of that, is there? In this eclectic jumble there
will surely be feelings, sensations, emotions
and moments of happiness that you, too, have
felt and still feel. And you have your own stock
of memories which ask nothing better than to
resurface, keep you company, and support you in
all you have yet to do. I have learnt to recognize
them for what they are: the pleasing milestones
of our lives. All at once they become so much
richer and more interesting than we think. And
above all, tell yourself that none of all that can
ever be taken away from you.

Turning the page

There's no magic about it, I wrote to the friend I'm addressing in this letter. No, but nonetheless it is of the utmost importance. Who am 'I', beyond the superficial definitions that might be made of me: physical appearance, character in broad outline, relationships with other people, professional and personal connections, ties with family and friends, reputation, commitments, the networks to which I belong – beyond such definitions, which may be accurate but are also artificially constructed and deceptive, who, in a more profound sense, am I? And the 'I' which is our wealth consists of opening up to the world – an aptitude for observation, an empathy with life, an ability to be at one with reality. 'I' am not only a thinking, acting being, but one with the capacity for feeling and experience, in accordance with the laws of a subterranean energy that is always being renewed. Stripped entirely of curiosity, empathy, desire, the ability to feel distress and pleasure, what would the 'I' who also thinks, talks and acts be?

I wanted to track down the imperceptible force that animates and defines us. It depends on the story of our lives, of course, but it does not hark back to the past; even if we ignore the fact, it is the quintessence and justification of all that we do now and will do in the future. 'I' would not be what I am if certain events that channelled the course of my life had not occurred, or if 'I' had not had the chance of feeling this or that emotion, responding to such and such an occasion, having this, that or the other physical experience.

This book is a plea for us to recognize not simply the small, artless influence of childhood but the whole complex affective domain that forms and continues to form us, sensitive beings that we are. A plea for us not to be simply obsessed by targets – careers to be created, enterprises to be undertaken, profits to be secured – while losing sight of the 'I' who entered the arena in the first place. A plea for us to understand that the profound engine of curiosity is at work in us, sustaining the ever-renewed feat of living, the benevolent and empathetic or critical and constituent view that 'I' take of the world all around me.

We should give ourselves time to compile an intimate anthology of sensuality that can nonetheless be shared, a fundamental substrate of the 'human condition'. In using that expression and many others (think of the 'vale of tears' that existence on this earth is supposed to be!), we always approach the scalding experience of pain and the crucial fact of death. Yes, but the human condition also implies the capacity for longing and desire, the ability to feel, to be moved, touched, full of emotion, and to communicate all that to others who understand this common language.

'I' am also made up of what I remember, but

what rules govern our selection of memories? That selection operates without the intervention of the will, and psychoanalysis has a great deal to say about the reasons for needing to forget, although not all lost memories are due to the working of the unconscious mind. The incident itself is lost, but the essence of it remains, making its mark on the body, and that essence will reappear in response to the fleeting magic of a reminiscence, the thrill of a sensation, the surprisingly acute and sometimes incomprehensible strength of an emotion. What calls it forth if not that burning internal voice, the vital dynamo that we do not even know we have developed over the course of time? The memory itself may have gone, but the sensual memory of the body still speaks of it. We are made of material provided with sensors which record the tenacious impressions that guard and guide us. We would be paralysed by too many memories. But the prototypes of what, in the great range of potential emotions, really touches us remain.

We are not so far from Proust here. However, the taste of a madeleine does not in itself revive a memory. That comes of sensory unrest recalling the same sensual turmoil in childhood, thanks to a ceremonial in which the essence of it all – a concentration of the confined atmosphere, the exceptional character of the incident, the time, the person of the child's aunt, the tea, the madeleine – was about to take wing, like a well-aimed arrow flying through the air, and take root for ever in the sweet, slightly insipid odour of a little sponge cake, that is to say the odour of the sensations experienced at the time, which was perhaps the aspect best suited to condense the perpetual vitality of all these elements combined for the child concerned.

In a way each of us provides evidence of the sensualism elaborated by the French philosopher Condillac: The world exists through our senses before existing in more ordered fashion in our minds, and we should do all we can to preserve the creative faculty of sense throughout our lives: seeing, hearing, observing, understanding, touching, caressing, smelling, inhaling, tasting, exercising the faculty of 'taste', for everyone, for others, for life itself.

Some References

Films and TV Series:

- *Agatha Christie's Poirot*, British TV series, (David Suchet).

- *A High Wind in Jamaica*, Alexander Mackendrick, 1965.

- *Alien*, Ridley Scott, 1979.

- *Ally McBeal*, American TV series by David E. Kelley.

- *Amarcord*, Federico Fellini, 1974.

- Animal documentary in the series *Chroniques de l'Afrique sauvage* (Dying Cheetah).

— *Bad Day at Black Rock*, John Sturges, 1955
    (Spencer Tracy).

— *Dark Passage*, Delmer Daves, 1947
    (Agnes Moorehead).

— *Dune*, David Lynch, 1984.

— *Frankenstein*, James Whale, 1931.

— *Gone with the Wind*, Victor Fleming, 1939.

— *House*, American TV series, David Shore.

— *King Kong*, Merian C. Cooper and Ernest B.
    Schoedsack, 1933.

— *Kiss Me Deadly*, Robert Aldrich, 1955.

— *Kiss of Death*, Henry Hathaway, 1979
    (Richard Widmark).

— *Morse*, British TV series by Colin Dexter.

— *My Darling Clementine*, John Ford, 1946
    (Henry Fonda).

— *NCIS* (Naval Criminal Investigative Service),
    American TV series by Donald P. Bellisario and
    Don McGill.

— *Out of Africa*, Sydney Pollack, 1985.

— *Peau d'Âne*, Jacques Demy, 1970.

— *Queen Kelly*, Erich von Stroheim, 1928.

— *Taxi Driver*, Martin Scorsese, 1976 (Robert De Niro).

— *The Age of Innocence*, Martin Scorsese, 1993.

— *The Bear*, Jean-Jacques Annaud, 1988
     (Tchéky Karyo).

— *The Dead*, John Huston, 1987.

— *The Ghost and Mrs Muir*, Joseph L. Mankiewicz, 1947
     (Gene Tierney).

— *The Incredible Shrinking Man*, Jack Arnold, 1957.

— *The Navigator*, Buster Keaton and Donald Crisp,
     1924 (Buster Keaton).

— *The Treasure of the Sierra Madre*, John Huston, 1948.

— *The Wolf of the Malveneurs*, Guillaume Radot, 1943.

— *What's Eating Gilbert Grape*, Lasse Hallström, 1993
     (Leonardo DiCaprio).

— *Without Apparent Motive*, Philippe Labro, 1971 (Jean-
     Louis Trintignant).

Other References:

— Dorothy Baker, *Young Man with a Horn*,
     1938 (Bix Beiderbecke, 1903–31).

— Simone de Beauvoir, *Le Deuxième Sexe*
     (The Second Sex), 1949.

— *Cahiers du cinéma*, journal founded in 1951 by André Bazin, Jacques Doniol-Valcroze and Joseph-Marie Lo Duca.

— Jean Cocteau, *L'Aigle à deux têtes* (The Eagle with Two Heads), 1947.

— Frank Herbert, *Dune*, 1965.

— Patricia Highsmith, *A Dog's Ransom*, 1972.

— Mary Ann Shaffer, and Annie Barrows *The Guernsey Literary and Potato Peel Pie Society*, 2009.

— Pieter Jansz Saenredam, Flemish painter (1597–1665).

— Franz Schubert, *Die Winterreise*, cycle of lieder.

— Jean Vauthier, *La Nouvelle Mandragore* (The New Mandrake), after Niccoló Macchiavelli's *La Mandragola*, play directed by Gérard Philipe in 1952 at the Théâtre National Populaire.

What activities offer you the sweetness of life?